THE SPACE RACE

On November 3, 1957, the Soviet spacecraft *Sputnik 2* was launched into orbit, carrying the first earthling to enter space. This was neither a man nor a woman, but a small mongrel dog named Laika. Her flight proved that it was possible for a living thing to at least enter space and survive. There was no way to return her to Earth, and eventually she died in space.

The early spacecraft were not very reliable: many of them exploded shortly after liftoff or failed to return to Earth safely. At first they were thought to be too dangerous to carry people, so the first astronauts were animals – monkeys, dogs, and mice. Many of them did not return to Earth alive, if at all.

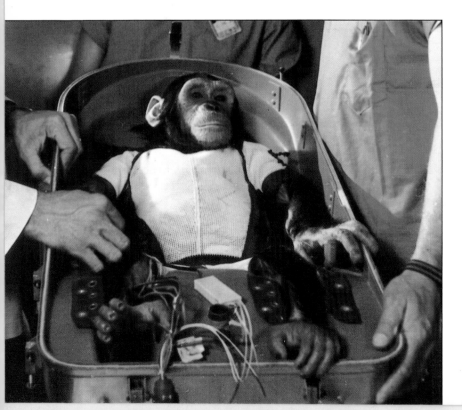

LEFT Ham the chimpanzee was launched into space in 1961. He returned to Earth alive in spite of several problems during the flight.

RIGHT An astronaut at work outside the cargo bay of an orbiting space shuttle, far above the clouds.

LIVING DANGEROUSLY

ASTRONAUTS

JONATHAN BURCH

GEC GARRETT EDUCATIONAL CORPORATION

LIVING **DANGEROUSLY**

ASTRONAUTS
DIVERS
FIREFIGHTERS
PILOTS
RACING DRIVERS
STUNT PERFORMERS

Cover: Astronaut Bruce McCandless walking in space with the aid of a Manned Maneuvering Unit.

Edited by Rebecca Stefoff

© 1992 by Garrett Educational Corporation
First published in the United States in 1992 by
Garrett Educational Corporation
130 East 13th Street, Ada, OK 74820

© 1991 Wayland Publishers, Limited
First published in 1991 by Wayland
Publishers, Limited

Printed in Italy. Bound in USA.

Library of Congress Cataloging-in-Publication Data

Burch. Jonathan.
    Astronauts/Jonathan Burch.
        p. cm.—(Living dangerously)
    Includes index.
    Summary: Discusses the different stages of space travel,
the difficult training undergone by astronauts, and the dangers
they face in space.
    ISBN 1-56074-041-8
    1. Astronauts—Juvenile literature. 2. Astronautics—
Juvenile literature. [1. Astronauts. 2. Astronautics.]
I. Title. II. Series.
TL793.B84   1991
629.45'0092'2—dc20   91-45925
                                            CIP
                                            AC

CONTENTS

THE SPACE RACE 4

THE RIGHT STUFF 6

LIFTOFF! 9

LIFE IN SPACE 12

LANDING ON THE MOON 19

DOWN TO EARTH.................................22

THE SPACE SHUTTLE.........................25

GLOSSARY 30

INDEX...31

THE SPACE RACE

On November 3, 1957, the Soviet spacecraft *Sputnik 2* was launched into orbit, carrying the first earthling to enter space. This was neither a man nor a woman, but a small mongrel dog named Laika. Her flight proved that it was possible for a living thing to at least enter space and survive. There was no way to return her to Earth, and eventually she died in space.

The early spacecraft were not very reliable: many of them exploded shortly after liftoff or failed to return to Earth safely. At first they were thought to be too dangerous to carry people, so the first astronauts were animals – monkeys, dogs, and mice. Many of them did not return to Earth alive, if at all.

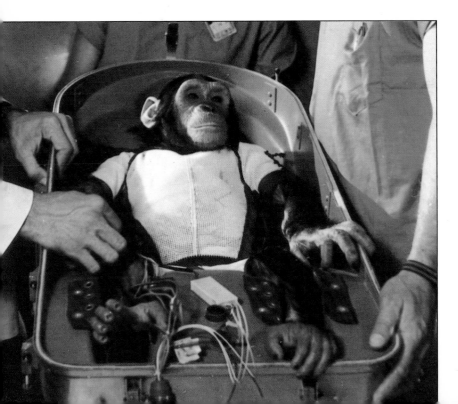

LEFT Ham the chimpanzee was launched into space in 1961. He returned to Earth alive in spite of several problems during the flight.

RIGHT An astronaut at work outside the cargo bay of an orbiting space shuttle, far above the clouds.

ABOVE **A group of astronauts training to put out a fire. A major fire inside a spacecraft would be disastrous.**

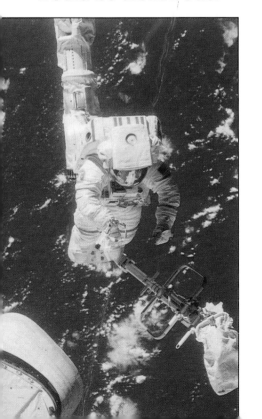

In spite of the great dangers, the USA and USSR were very eager to launch a person into space, to prove that it could be done. In April 1961, the Soviet space team decided to risk it. They launched the cosmonaut Yuri Gagarin aboard *Vostok 1*, and in a successful flight lasting 108 minutes he became the first human not only to enter space, but also to orbit the Earth.

Over the next few years the USA and the USSR made great efforts to send more people up into space, and each nation was eager to prove itself better than the other. These were the days of the "space race," when astronauts and cosmonauts took great risks in order "to boldly go where no one had gone before." Looking back at some of the near-disasters and narrow escapes, it is surprising that more people have not been killed in space travel.

5

THE **RIGHT STUFF**

What does it take to be an astronaut? First, your body must be in perfect shape in order to withstand the stresses of space travel. Every aspect of your health and fitness is investigated in the most thorough of medical examinations. If anything is found to be less than perfect, you cannot become an astronaut.

Second, you must be highly intelligent. Before you can be launched into space, you will need to learn and understand many things about space travel. It is vital that you have a detailed knowledge of your spacecraft and flight plan, so that you can solve any problems that may crop up during the mission.

Cosmonauts training in a tank of water. Underwater training is good practice for the weightless conditions of space.

Third, you must be very cool and quick-thinking in an emergency. You will be tested to find out how you would behave in a crisis: any hint that you would crack under the strain, and you will be rejected.

Finally, you and your family must be prepared to accept the great risks you will be taking. This is probably harder for your family. During a mission you will have so much to do that your mind will be taken off the dangers. Meanwhile your family can only wait anxiously on the ground, hoping your flight will end in triumph rather than disaster.

Toughening up

The difficult selection tests are only the beginning of the ordeal that will prepare you for life as an astronaut. You must be trained to cope with all the unpleasant and difficult conditions that you might encounter on your journey into space. During this training, you will be spun and tumbled around until you are sick and dizzy. Your heart and lungs will be exercised almost to the point of failure. You will have to put up with intense vibration, extremes of heat and cold, lack of air, and deafening noises. You will even be locked in a tiny chamber so that you become used to isolation and confinement.

One training machine that you will come to hate is the centrifuge. This teaches you to withstand the very high G-force you will experience on your mission. G-force is the force you feel when you are speeded up or slowed down. It pushes you back into the

A Soviet controller keeps a careful watch on the television pictures of a cosmonaut undergoing centrifuge training. The cosmonaut is being whirled around in the compartment at the top right of the picture.

seat of a car when it accelerates quickly, or makes you lurch forward if the car brakes suddenly. When traveling into space, you will experience much higher G-force than you would in a car. The centrifuge creates the effect of G-force by spinning you around at high speed. This makes you feel many times heavier than normal. Sometimes the centrifuge makes you faint, as the blood is forced out of your head just like water from the clothes in a spin-drier.

Danger Fact

In January 1967, the crew of *Apollo 1* were burned alive when a fire broke out in their space capsule. People were prepared for deaths to occur during space travel, but these three astronauts were killed as they tested their space capsule on the ground, and everyone was shocked by the tragedy.

LIFTOFF!

What is it like to be an astronaut waiting in the rocket for liftoff? You are lying in your seat inside the space capsule, high above the ground. The rocket below you is loaded with fuel and can explode with the force of a small nuclear bomb if anything goes wrong.

The top of a *Saturn V* rocket as it lifts off the launch pad. The pencil-shaped escape rocket at the top is designed to save astronauts in an emergency.

Tension mounts as the countdown
reaches its final stages. Several seconds
before liftoff, the rocket's motors are ignited.
There is a deafening roar and the space

LEFT **The launch of** *Apollo 16*, **the fifth successful Moon landing mission.**

capsule shakes violently. The rocket is held down on the launch pad so that its motors can develop maximum thrust before liftoff. The countdown continues: ". . . five . . . four . . . three . . . two . . . one . . . zero. Liftoff! We have liftoff!" The rocket is released from the launch pad and you are jolted in your seat as it surges upward.

Faster and faster the rocket soars into the air, leaving a huge cloud of billowing smoke and fire behind it. The high G-force pushes you down into your seat and makes you feel weak, but you must remain alert in case anything goes wrong. The launch pad has become a small speck far below you as you rise through the clouds.

Then, only a few minutes later, the motors stop and the rocket falls away beneath you. It has launched you into space and its job is done. Suddenly everything is quiet – the roaring and shaking have stopped. Your journey into space has taken only about ten minutes.

Danger Fact

In September 1983, the crew of the Soviet *Soyuz T-10* mission had a very narrow escape in a launch pad explosion. All seemed well until twenty-five seconds before liftoff, when their rocket caught fire. An emergency rocket was meant to take the crew away from the danger, but it had been damaged by the blaze. Fortunately, the emergency rocket was launched just as the *Soyuz T-10* exploded in a huge fireball. The cosmonauts had been saved in the nick of time.

LIFE IN SPACE

On Earth we are protected from the dangers of space by the atmosphere. Outside the Earth's atmosphere the conditions are too harsh for a human being to survive. Spacecraft have life-support systems to keep the astronauts inside them alive. They must be very reliable because the astronauts' lives depend on them completely.

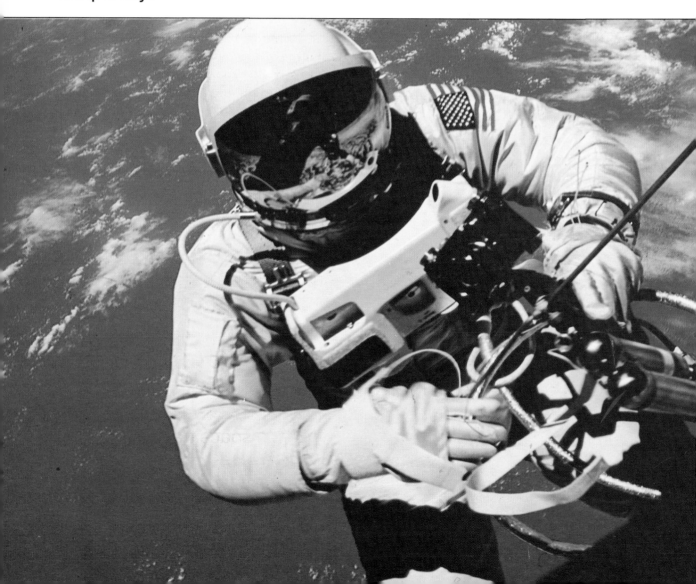

There is no air in space: it is a vacuum. The life-support system must maintain the air pressure inside the spacecraft and provide oxygen for the astronauts to breathe. Without the life-support system, they would not only suffocate but their blood would boil, their lungs would collapse, and their bodies would blow up like balloons.

Although the Sun provides the heat and light we need to live, it also gives out very harmful rays. On the Earth we are protected from these rays by the atmosphere, though they can still give us sunburn if we are not careful. Astronauts in space are exposed to much stronger rays from the Sun, even inside their space capsule. They have to wear helmets with reflective visors to shield their eyes and protect them from blindness.

In space the heat of the Sun is very strong. The side of the spacecraft facing the Sun will get very hot, while the side facing away will be extremely cold. On its journey to the Moon, the *Apollo* spacecraft used to turn around very slowly – like a chicken on a spit – to even out the heating from the Sun. This was known as "barbecue mode."

Meteorites are lumps of rock of various sizes that fly around in space. They are not dangerous to people on Earth. Any meteorites that come close are burned up in the atmosphere, and we call them "shooting stars." However, meteorites are a deadly menace to space travelers. Any meteorite that hits a spacecraft would hit many times faster than a bullet, and could cause severe damage.

LEFT **Astronaut Ed White is bathed in sunlight as he floats outside his spacecraft. He was the first American to walk in space.**

13

Spacecraft have special shells to protect them, but these only prevent damage from meteorites weighing less than an ounce. Anything bigger than that would cause disaster, but fortunately larger meteorites are very rare and haven't yet been encountered.

As we launch more and more things into space, the amount of "space junk" left there is increasing all the time, and this could cause problems for space travelers in the future.

Weightlessness

Perhaps the strangest thing about being in space is the feeling of weightlessness. On the Earth the pull of gravity holds us firmly on the ground. When orbiting the Earth or traveling to the Moon, astronauts do not feel such a force, so they float around with no sense of up or down.

Although it can be fun when you have become used to it, weightlessness creates a number of problems. At first, many astronauts find that it gives them a feeling like seasickness. As well as being unpleasant, this can be dangerous: vomiting in a spacesuit could block the air supply and suffocate the astronaut.

Weightlessness also means that there are hazards involved in simply having a meal. Drinks must be sucked in through tubes – they would float out of an open container like a cup. Foods that produce crumbs can be dangerous. Astronaut John Young got into trouble with Mission

The shuttle spacesuit as worn by astronauts.

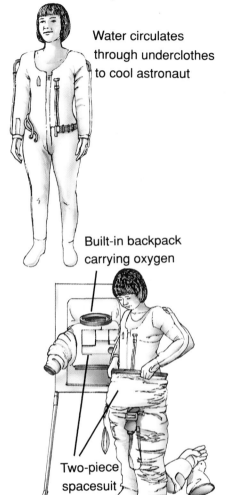

Water circulates through underclothes to cool astronaut

Built-in backpack carrying oxygen

Two-piece spacesuit

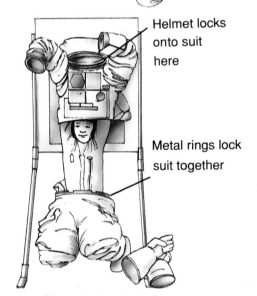

Helmet locks onto suit here

Metal rings lock suit together

Gloves lock onto suit

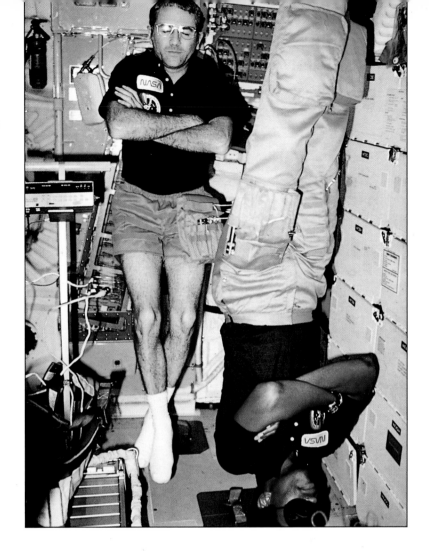

RIGHT Two astronauts resting inside the space shuttle. They have different ideas of up and down!

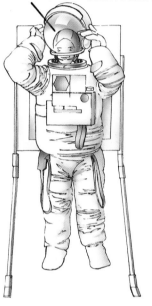

Cap with microphone and headphones for talking to other crew and mission control

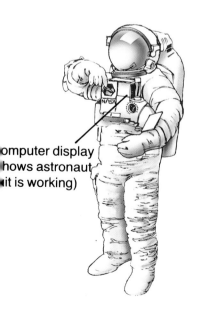

Computer display shows astronaut it is working)

Control when they found that he had smuggled a corned beef sandwich into space with him! They were afraid that crumbs from the sandwich would float around inside the space capsule and cause problems.

One of the more serious effects of weightlessness is that it causes a person's bones and muscles to waste away. This is a danger for astronauts who spend long periods of time in space, like the cosmonauts on board the USSR's *Mir* space station. They have to do a great deal of exercise to maintain their strength.

Space walking

Sometimes astronauts need to leave the safety of their spacecraft and float freely outside it. This is called space walking, or extra-vehicular activity (EVA). During EVA astronauts wear spacesuits to protect them from the harsh conditions in space. Nevertheless, they are exposed to very great danger all the time they are outside. Spacesuits have many protective layers, but they are much less strong than the metal shell of a spacecraft. A collision with all but the tiniest of meteorites would make a hole in a spacesuit, so some astronauts carry puncture repair kits in case of emergency.

RIGHT **Astronaut Robert Stewart floats freely in space. He can move around with the aid of a backpack called a Manned Maneuvering Unit (MMU).**

LEFT **In 1984, Svetlana Savitskaya became the first woman to walk in space. She stayed outside her spacecraft for three and a half hours.**

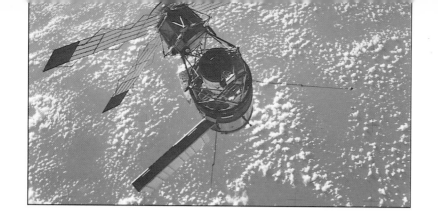

The USA's *Skylab* space station in orbit above the Earth.

Space stations

Space stations such as *Mir* or the USA's *Skylab* are launched into long-term orbit around the Earth. They provide the facilities for astronauts to stay in space for many months at a time. The astronauts are ferried to and from the space stations in space capsules launched by rockets. They spend their time performing scientific experiments and studying the Earth and stars.

The Soviets are the masters of long-term space station missions. In December 1988, cosmonauts Vladimir Titov and Musakhi Manarov returned to Earth after spending a whole year on board the *Mir* space station.

Danger Fact

In March 1965, the cosmonaut Alexei Leonov became the first person to venture outside his capsule for a space walk. While he was outside, however, his spacesuit ballooned out and prevented him from getting back in again! He was stuck outside his spacecraft and became dangerously weak and tired from trying to force his way in. Eventually, he had no choice but to risk letting most of the air out of his suit. This made it smaller and he managed to squeeze back in through the hatch.

The giant *Saturn V* rockets were the largest ever built. They stood 360 feet high on the launch pad and weighed nearly 3,000 tons. Their motors made an earth-shattering roar and gave out so much heat that they used to melt the launch pad during liftoff! These rockets were used in the *Apollo* Moon missions, which were the most ambitious and complicated space journeys ever undertaken.

Each *Saturn V* rocket launched an *Apollo* spacecraft, which was designed to carry three men to the Moon and back. The astronauts were contained in a small compartment called the command module. This was attached to the service module, which contained the motors used for maneuvering the spacecraft when it was in space. The final part of the spacecraft was the lunar module, which was used to actually land on the Moon. It was 23 feet tall

Edwin Aldrin sets up a piece of equipment on the Moon. The lunar module is behind him.

and had legs that made it look a little like a strange kind of insect. Of the huge *Saturn V* vehicles, only the command modules ever returned to Earth intact; the other parts of the spacecraft were all discarded along the way.

The 250,000-mile journey to the Moon took three days, and the astronauts spent the time in the cramped command module. They had no toilet, and had to make do with special diapers and plastic bags.

When the *Apollo* spacecraft were in orbit around the Moon, two of the astronauts climbed into the lunar module for the trip to the surface. Their companion stayed in the command module to wait for their return. The lunar module had a descent motor to control its landing. It could hover above the Moon while the astronauts chose a suitable place to land, but it had only enough fuel for a few minutes' flight.

In 1969, Neil Armstrong and Edwin Aldrin became the first astronauts to land on the Moon. Their trip nearly ended in disaster because there were too many large boulders around for them to land safely.

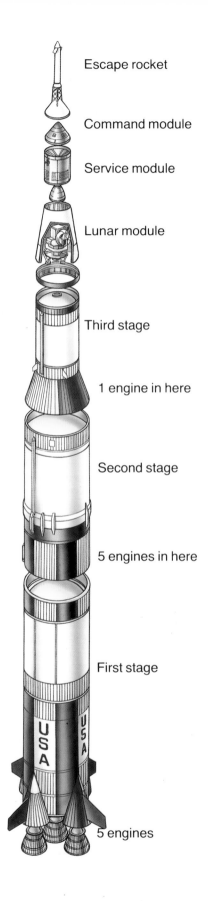

Escape rocket

Command module

Service module

Lunar module

Third stage

1 engine in here

Second stage

5 engines in here

First stage

5 engines

RIGHT **The *Apollo 11* lunar module is seen from the command module, returning from its landing on the Moon. The Earth is 250,000 miles away!**

LEFT AND BELOW **A *Saturn V* rocket and the *Apollo* command and service modules.**

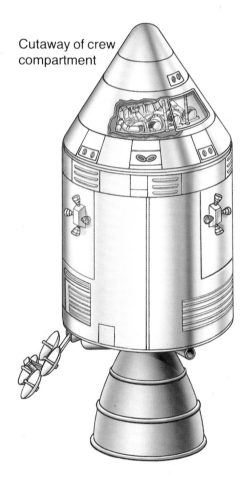

Cutaway of crew compartment

BOTTOM LEFT **The later *Apollo* missions had "moon buggies" for exploring the Moon.**

They were running out of fuel, and their lunar module's computer was nearly overloaded. Fortunately they found a suitable place to land just in time. They landed on the Moon with only about twenty seconds' worth of fuel left!

When the time came to leave the Moon, the two astronauts got back into the lunar module to prepare for takeoff. Their lives depended on the lunar module's ascent motor: if it had failed they would have been stranded on the Moon with no hope of rescue. Fortunately the ascent motor never failed during the *Apollo* missions. The two astronauts were carried up in the top half of the lunar module, leaving its legs behind on the Moon. Once in orbit around the Moon, the lunar module had to dock with the command module, so that the two astronauts could rejoin their companion ready for the trip back to Earth. It must have been a great relief for him to see the others after orbiting the Moon on his own for so long.

DOWN TO EARTH

As they return to Earth, astronauts face their last great danger: re-entry into the atmosphere. As they reach the atmosphere, the fastest space capsules are traveling at about 25,000 mph – more than a hundred times faster than a Formula One racing car! At such an enormous speed it is vital for a space capsule to hit the atmosphere at just the right angle. Too narrow an angle, and the capsule will "bounce" off the atmosphere and fly off into outer space. Too steep an angle, and it will burn up like a shooting star.

An *Apollo* space capsule re-entering the Earth's atmosphere.

Splashdown! The *Apollo 16* command module lands in the ocean. Soviet cosmonauts prefer to come down onto dry land.

As the capsule enters the atmosphere, it is heated up to a very high temperature by friction with the air. The capsule is protected by a heat shield that glows white-hot, but the capsule shakes violently as it is buffeted by the air. Through the small windows the astronauts can see nothing but the white-hot glow. They experience huge G-force as their capsule slows down.

23

This is a very tense period for the people waiting on the ground because they lose radio contact with the astronauts during re-entry. Everybody breathes a sigh of relief when the capsule appears high in the sky and its parachutes are released. Finally, the space capsule floats down supported by its parachutes and splashes down into the sea. The astronauts must wait inside for the recovery team to pick them up.

A helicopter recovers the space capsule of Alan Shepard, the first American in space.

Danger Fact

After their *Voshkod 2* mission, cosmonauts Pavel Belyayev and Alexei Leonov landed 1,250 miles off target, in deep snow in the middle of a forest. They spent a night in freezing conditions, surrounded by a pack of hungry wolves, before being rescued the next morning!

THE **SPACE SHUTTLE**

The USA's space shuttle is a cross between a rocket and an airplane. It takes off vertically like a rocket, but lands horizontally like an airplane. At liftoff, the shuttle rides piggyback on an enormous external fuel tank, which feeds the shuttle's main engines. Fixed to the side of the fuel tank are two booster rockets, which add to the thrust of the shuttle's own engines. The whole thing looks like a bundle of fireworks. Taking off in the shuttle is known to astronauts as "riding the stack."

***Discovery* lifts off from the launch pad.**

LEFT *Challenger* **orbits the Earth with its cargo bay doors open.**

After launch, the external fuel tank and booster rockets stay fixed to the shuttle until their fuel is used up; then they are released. The boosters float down into the ocean on parachutes; they can be recovered and used again.

The space shuttle has a large cargo bay that can be used for a variety of things: performing scientific experiments, carrying satellites up into orbit, or even fetching old satellites from orbit and returning them to Earth. It is much more comfortable inside the shuttle than it was in the early spacecraft. There is a wide range of food, a toilet, and plenty of room.

The shuttle is protected from the intense heat of re-entry into the atmosphere by heat-resistant tiles. After re-entry it glides down and lands on a runway like a normal airplane.

BELOW *Discovery* **glides in to land after a four-day mission.**

Disaster

On January 28, 1986, the *Challenger* space shuttle rose majestically from its launch pad and climbed into the air. It was the twenty-fifth shuttle mission and the first to carry a non-astronaut – the teacher Christa McAuliffe.

As it lifted off from the launch pad, nobody noticed a small puff of smoke coming out of the side of one of the booster rockets. Next to the huge clouds of smoke and flame coming from the main engines, it may not have seemed important to anyone who had noticed it, yet it was to spell disaster for *Challenger*. Seventy-three seconds into the flight, the shuttle exploded in a massive fireball. The whole crew of seven people – five men and two women – lost their lives. Some of them may have survived the explosion, but they couldn't escape from the wreckage as it fell back to the Earth.

Disaster! *Challenger's* rocket boosters fly off out of control as the shuttle disappears in a huge fireball.

This fragment of *Challenger*'s wreckage was recovered from the seabed. It still bears part of the space shuttle's name.

What had gone wrong? One of the booster rockets had sprung a leak, allowing a jet of flame to escape through the side. This had cut through part of the shuttle like a blowtorch, causing it to break apart and explode. Some engineers had been worried that this might happen, but their warnings had been ignored.

Following the *Challenger* disaster, no US space shuttles were launched until 1988 – they were being made safer to try to avoid another tragedy.

What can we learn from the *Challenger* disaster? Perhaps one of the most important lessons is that we mustn't take space travel for granted. There have been great advances since the early days of the space race, but space travel is still very dangerous. Before he died in the *Apollo 1* fire, the astronaut Virgil Grissom had said the following words: "If we die we want people to accept it . . . the conquest of space is worth the risk." Do you think it is worth the risk?

GLOSSARY

Apollo   Any of a series of manned US spacecraft designed to explore the Moon and surrounding space.

Ascent   Upward movement.

Astronaut   Someone who is trained to travel in space.

Atmosphere   The layer of air surrounding the Earth.

Capsule   The compartment of a rocket in which astronauts travel into space and return to Earth.

Cosmonaut   A Soviet space traveler.

Countdown   The time remaining before a rocket is launched.

Descent   Downward movement.

Dock   To link together in space.

External   Outside.

G-force   The force you feel when you are accelerated or slowed down.

Gravity   The force with which an object like the Earth or Moon pulls other objects toward itself.

Heat shield   The shell that protects a space capsule from burning up as it re-enters the Earth's atmosphere.

Launch pad   The structure that holds a rocket in position before it sets off on its journey into space.

Liftoff   The moment when a rocket rises from the launch pad and starts its journey into space.

Lunar   To do with the Moon.

Maneuvering   Moving in a planned and precise way.

Orbit   The process of a spacecraft or other object traveling around the Earth or Moon.

Re-entry   The time when a space capsule comes back into the Earth's atmosphere from space.

Rocket   A vehicle that launches astronauts up into space.

Satellite   An unmanned space vehicle that orbits the Earth.

Space   The huge emptiness outside the Earth's atmosphere. Space is never-ending, and it contains all the stars we see in the night sky.

Space race   The time when the USA and the USSR were competing with each other to be the best at space travel.

Thrust   The force produced by a rocket motor.

Vacuum   An empty space with nothing – not even air – in it.

INDEX

The numbers in **bold** refer to captions.

Aldrin, Edwin **19**, 20
Apollo missions **11**, 13, 19, 20, 21, **23**, 29
Armstrong, Neil 20
Atmosphere 12, 13, 22, 23

"Barbecue mode" 13
Booster rockets 25, 27, 28, 29

Centrifuges 7, 8
Challenger **27**, 28, 29
Command modules 19, 20, 21, **23**
Cosmonauts 5, **6**, **8**, 11, 15, 18, **23**, 24
Countdown 10, 11

Discovery **25**, **27**

Explosions 4, 9, 11, 28, 29

Fire **5**, 8, 11, 23, 28, 29
Flight plans 6

Gagarin, Yuri 5
G-force 7, 8, 11, 23
Gravity 14
Grissom, Virgil 29

Hazards 8, 9, 14, 16, 28, 29

Laika 4
Landing
    on Earth **23**, 24, 25, 27
    on the Moon **11**, 19-21
Launch pads **9**, 11, 19, **25**, 28
Life-support systems 12, 13
Liftoff 4, 9-11, 19, 25
Lunar module 19, 20, 21

Manarov, Musakhi 18
McAuliffe, Christa 28
Medical examinations 6
Meteorites 13, 14, 16
Mir 15, 18
Mission Control 14
Moon **11**, 14, 19, 20, 21

Orbit 4, 5, 14, 18, 21, 27

Parachutes 24, 27

Radio contact 24
Recovery teams 24
Re-entry 22, 24, 27
Rockets 9, 10, 11, 18, 19, **21**, 25

Satellites 27
Saturn V **9**, 19, 20, **21**
Savitskaya, Svetlana **16**
Scientific experiments 18, 27
Skylab 18
Soyuz T-10 11
Space capsules 8, 9, 10, 13, 15, 18, 22, 23, 24
Spacecraft 4, **5**, 6, 12, 13, 14, 16, 18, 19, 20, 27
"Space junk" 14
Space shuttles 4, **15**, 25-9
Space stations 15, 18

Space walking **13**, 16, 18
Splashdown **23**, 24
Sputnik 2 4

Stewart, Robert **17**
Titov, Vladimir 18
Training **6**, 7-8

Vostok 1 5

Weightlessness **6**, 14-15